GW00854168

Published by
Hal Leonard Europe
A Music Sales / Hal Leonard Joint Venture Company
14-15 Berners Street, London W1T 3LJ, UK.

Exclusive Distributors:
Music Sales Limited
Distribution Centre, Newmarket Road,
Bury St Edmunds, Suffolk IP33 3YB, UK.

Order No. HLE90003815
ISBN: 978-1-84938-002-7
This book © Copyright 2010 Hal Leonard Europe

Printed in the EU

Your Guarantee of Quality
As publishers, we strive to produce every book
to the highest commercial standards.
This book has been carefully designed to make playing from
it a real pleasure.
Particular care has been given to specifying acid-free,
neutral-sized paper made from pulps which have not
been elemental chlorine bleached.
This pulp is from farmed sustainable forests and was
produced with special regard for the environment.
Throughout, the printing and binding have been planned
to ensure a sturdy, attractive publication which should
give years of enjoyment.
If your copy fails to meet our high standards,
please inform us and we will gladly replace it.

www.musicsales.com

Good Morning Baltimore

Words & Music by Marc Shaiman & Scott Wittman

rhy - thm of town starts call - ing me down. It's like a mes - sage from
rats on the streets all dance 'round my feet. They seem to say, "Tra - cy, it's

high a - bove _____ Oh, oh, oh. Pull - ing me out to the
up to you." _____ So, oh, oh. Don't hold me back, 'cause to -

smiles and the streets that I love. Good morn - ing, Bal - ti - more!
day all my dreams will come true. Good morn - ing, Bal - ti - more!

Ev - 'ry day's like an o - pen door. Ev - 'ry night is a
There's the flash - er who lives next door. There's the bum on his

fan - ta - sy.   Ev - 'ry sound's like   a   sym - pho - ny.
bar - room stool.   They wish me luck on   my   way   to school.

Good morn - ing, Bal - ti - more!   And some day when I

take to the floor,   the world's gon - na wake up and _ see

Bal - ti - more and me.

me.   I know ev - 'ry step.   I

know ev - 'ry song.   I know there's a place where   I   be - long.   I

see all those par - ty lights shin - ing a - head. So some - one in - vite me be -

-fore I drop dead! _____ So, oh, oh.

Give me a chance, 'cause when I start to dance I'm a mo - vie __ star. __

Oh, oh, oh. Some - thing in - side of me makes me move when

The Nicest Kids In Town

Words & Music by Marc Shaiman & Scott Wittman

once a month we have our "Ne-gro Day!" And I'm the man who keeps it

spin-nin' 'round, Mis-ter Corn-y Col-lins with the lat-est, great-est

Bal-ti-more sound!! So

ev-'ry af-ter-noon drop ev-'ry-thing. (Bop bee-ba, ba-

COUNCIL

21

ba - ba - ba - ba bee - ba) Who needs ___ to read and write when you can dance and sing? ___

(Bop - bee - ba, ba - ba - ba - ba - ba bee - ba) For - get a - bout your al - ge - bra and

cal - cu - lus. ___ You can al - ways do your home-work on the morn - ing bus. ___ Can't tell a

verb from a noun, they're the nic - est kids in town. ___ (Ooh ooo ___

ooh, mo - ny, mo - ny) who cares a - bout sleep when you can snooze in school? _ They'll

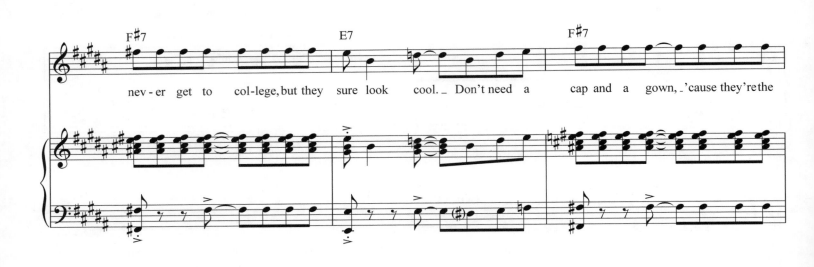

nev - er get to col - lege, but they sure look cool. _ Don't need a cap and a gown, _ 'cause they're the

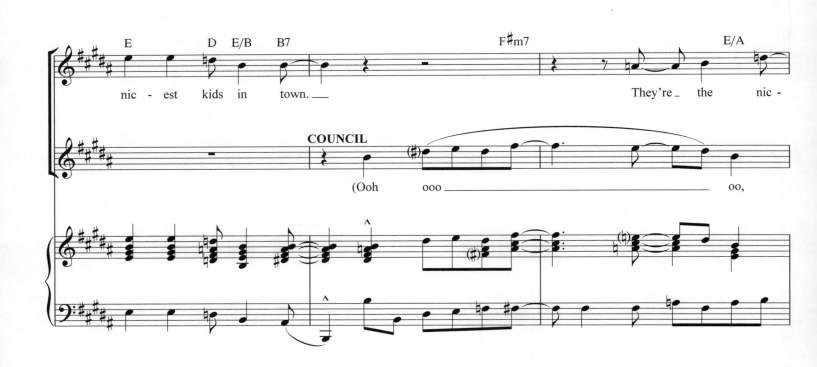

nic - est kids in town. ___   They're _ the nic -

(Ooh   ooo _____ oo,

Mama, I'm A Big Girl Now

Words & Music by Marc Shaiman & Scott Wittman

lose that laun-dry list of what you won't al - low, _____ 'cause, ma-ma, I'm a big girl now!

AMBER
Once up - on a time I used to play with toys, _____ but

now I'd rath - er play a - round with teen-age boys. _____ So, if I get a hick - ey, please don't

have a cow, _____ 'cause, ma-ma, I'm a big girl now!

PENNY
Ma, _____

28

CHORUS
Hey, ma-ma, say, ma-ma.

TRACY
Once up-on a time I was a shy young thing. ___ Could bare-ly walk and talk so much as dance and sing. ___ But let me hit the stage, I wan-na take my bow, ___ 'cause, ma-ma, I'm a big girl now!

AMBER
Wo - oh - oh - oh - oh!

Once up-on a time I used to dress up "Ken," ___ but now that I'm a wom-an I like

33

34

I Can Hear The Bells

Words & Music by Marc Shaiman & Scott Wittman

Slowly and freely

TRACY

I can — hear the bells. Well, don't cha — hear 'em chime?

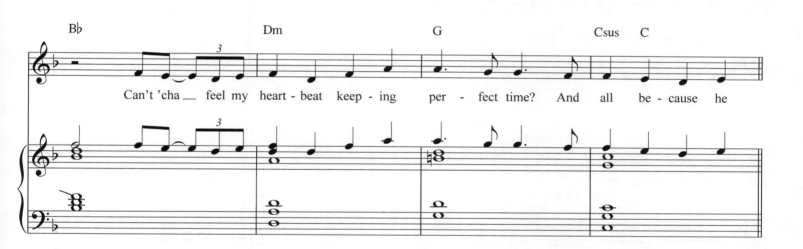

Can't 'cha — feel my heart-beat keep-ing per-fect time? And all be-cause he

Moderate Rock beat

touched me. He looked at ___ me and stared. Yes, he bumped me. My

primp, but __ won't be late be - cause round three's when we kiss in - side his car. Won't

go all the way, but I'll go pret - ty far. Then round four, he'll

ask me __ for my hand, and then round five, we'll book the __ wed - ding band, so by

round six, Am - ber, much to your sur - prise, this heav - y - weight cham - pi - on

39

walks me down the aisle.___ My moth-er starts to cry, but I can't see 'cause Link and I are French-

kiss - in'. Lis - ten! I can ___ hear the bells.___

I can ___ hear the bells. My head is reel - in'. I can ___ hear the bells. I

It Takes Two

Words & Music by Marc Shaiman & Scott Wittman

And so I will wait un-til that mo-ment _____ you de-
So please, dar-ling, choose me. ___ I don't wan-na _____ rule a-
So come clos-er, ba-by, ___ oh, and whis-per _____ in my

-cide _____ that I'm your man and you're my girl, ___ that
-lone. _____ Tell me I'm your king and you're my queen, that
ear _____ that you're my girl and I'm your boy, ___ that

I'm the sea and you're the pearl. It takes two, ___ ba-by, it ___ takes
no one else can come be-tween. It takes two, ___ ba-by, it ___ takes
you're my pride and I'm your joy, _____ that

two. _____

two. _____

45

Lan - ce - lot had Guin-e-vere. Miss-us Claus had old Saint Nick._

Ro - me - o had Ju - li - et,_____ and Liz, well, she has her Dick._ They

say it takes two to tan - go, but that tan - go's_ child's play._ So

D.S. al Coda

take me to the dance floor,_ and we'll twist the night a - way._____

46

CODA

I'm the sand and you're the tide. _ I'll be the groom if you'll be my bride. _ It takes two, __ ba - by, it __ takes two. _____ It takes two, _____ ba - by, It _____ takes two.

Welcome To The 60's

Words & Music by Marc Shaiman & Scott Wittman

TRACY, DYNAMITES & ENSEMBLE

wan - na set free. _ So let go, _____ go, go of the past ____ now. _ Say hel - lo _
asked me to dance. _ **T:** So let go, _____ go, go of the past ____ now. _ Say hel - lo _

_ to the love _ in your heart. _____ Yes, I know _ that the world's _ spin - ning fast _
_ to the light _ in your eyes. _____ Yes, I know _ that the world's _ spin - ning fast _

_ now. _ You got - ta get your - self a brand - new start. }
_ now, but you got - ta run the race to win the prize. }

Hey ma - ma, wel - come to the

six - ties! Oh - oh - oh - oh - oh. _____ Oh _

49

50

2

F/G   B♭ **DYNAMITES**   F   **TRACY**

___ yeah, yeah!   Wel - come to the rhy - thm of a brand-new day. __ Take your old-

Dm7   F/G   **TRACY & DYNAMITES**   B♭   **MR. PINKY'S STAFF**

- fash - ioned fears __ and just throw __ them a - way. __   You should add some col - or and a

F   Dm7   **DYNAMITES & ENSEMBLE**   G9sus   D/E

fresh new "do" 'cause it's time for a star who looks just like you. __

E   C♯   B/C♯   F♯   **JUDINE**

Don't-cha let no - bod - y try to

sfz

51

KAMILAH

steal your fun, __ 'cause a lit - tle touch of lip-stick nev - er hurt no one. __ The

G

fu - ture's got a mil - lion roads for you to choose, __ but you'll walk __

SHAYNA

__ a lit - tle tall - er in some high - heeled shoes. __ And

A7sus   A   Asus

once you find the style that make you feel like you, __ some - thing fresh, __

52

Run And Tell That

Words & Music by Marc Shaiman & Scott Wittman

whats's the use? ___ The dark - er the choc - 'late, the rich - er the taste. ___ And

that's where it's at... ___ ...now run and tell _____ that! (Run and tell

that!) Run and tell _____ that! (Run and tell that!)

SEAWEED

I can't see ___ why peo - ple dis - a - gree each time I tell them what I know is true. ___

SEAWEED &
ENSEMBLE

LI'L INEZ

I'm ti-red of cov-'rin' up all ___ my pride. _ So give me five on the black-hand side. I've got a new way of mov-in' and I got my own voice. So how can I help but to shout and re-joice? The peo-ple 'round here ___ can bare-ly pay their rent. ___ They're "try'n'" to make a dol-lar out-ta

65

Big, Blonde And Beautiful

Words & Music by Marc Shaiman & Scott Wittman

one day my grand-ma who was big and stout, _ she said you got-ta love your-self from

in - side out. And just as soon as I learned how to strut my fun - ky stuff, _ I

found out that the world at large can't get e - nough. So... bring on _ that

pe - can pie. _ Pour _ some sug - ar on it, sug - ar. Don't be shy. _ Scoop _

DIALOGUE

Look out, ___ old Bal - ti - more! ___ We're march - ing

74

75

76

Timeless To Me

Words & Music by Marc Shaiman & Scott Wittman

WILBUR
Styles keep a - chang - in'. The world's re - ar - rang - in', but

Ed - na, you're time - less to me. ____

there's no cure, so let this fe - ver rage. Some folks can't stand it, say

time is a ban - dit, but I take the op - po - site view. ___

___ 'Cause when I need a lift, time ___ brings a gift: an -

oth - er day with you. ___ A twist or a waltz, it's

83

pour me a teen-y ween-y tri - ple ___ and we can toast _ the fact we ain't dead yet! I can't stop eat-ing. Your hair - line's re - ced-ing. Soon there'll be noth-ing at all. _____ So, you'll wear a wig while I roast a pig. Hey! Pass that Ge - ri - tol! _

84

bor - ing you ain't! **BOTH** Some folks don't get it, but

we nev - er fret it 'cause we know that time is our friend. ___

And it's plain to see that

you're stuck with me un - til the bit - ter end. ___

87

Without Love

Words & Music by Marc Shaiman & Scott Wittman

Once I was a sim-ple girl, ___ then star-dom came to me. ___ But I was still a noth - ing, though a thou-sand fans may dis-a - gree. ___ Fame was just a pris - on, sign-ing au-to-graphs ___ a bore. ___ I did-n't have ___ a clue ___ till you came bang-ing on ___ my door ___ that with-out

95

96

97

98

102

I Know Where I've Been

Words & Music by Marc Shaiman & Scott Wittman

106

You Can't Stop The Beat

Words & Music by Marc Shaiman & Scott Wittman

-sons, girl, but you know___ you nev-er will.___ And you can try to stop___ my danc-ing feet, but I just___ can-not___ stand still.___ 'Cause the world___ keeps spin-ning 'round___ and 'round, and my heart's___ keep-ing time___ to the speed___ of sound. I was lost___ till I heard___ the drums,

TRACY & LINK

then I found my way _____ 'cause you can't stop the beat!

Ev - er since this old world be - gan, __ a wom - an found out if she shook it, she could

shake up a man. And so I'm gon - na shake and shim - my it the best that I can to - day,

_____ 'cause you can't stop the mo - tion of the o - cean or the

sun in the sky. You can won - der if you wan - na, but I nev - er ask why. And if you

try to hold me down, I'm gon - na spit in your eye ___ and say ___ that

you can't stop the beat! _____

PENNY You____ can't stop a riv-

-er as____ it rush - es out to sea.____ You can try____

____ to stop____ the hands____ of time, but ya know____ it____ just____ can't be.____

____ And if they try to stop____ us, Sea - weed, I'll call the

113

N - dou -ble- A - C - P! _____ 'Cause the world _____ keeps spin - ning 'round ___

and 'round, and my heart's ___ keep-ing time ___ to the speed ___ of sound. I was lost ___

___ till I heard ___ the drums, then I found my way _____ **PENNY & SEAWEED** 'cause

you can't stop the beat! Ev - er since we first saw the light, ___ a man and

114

'cause you can't stop the beat! _____

EDNA You can't stop my hap - pi - ness, 'cause I like ___

the way I am. ___ And you just ___ can't stop ___ my knife

Ev - er since this old world be - gan, __ a wom - an found out if she shook it, she could

shake up a man. And so I'm gon - na shake and shim - my it the best that I can __ to - day,

'cause you can't stop the mo - tion of the o - cean or the

sun in the sky. You can won - der if you wan - na, but I nev - er ask why. And if you

118

try to hold me down, I'm gon-na spit in your eye ___ and say ___ that

you can't stop the beat! ___

MOTORMOUTH
Oh, oh, oh, you ___ can't stop to-day ___ as it comes speed-

119

-ing down the track. ___ Child, yes - ter - day ___ is his-

- t'ry and it's nev - er com - ing back ___ 'cause to - mor-

Gb/Db   Db   Gb/Db   Db   Ab/Eb   Eb

- row is ___ a brand ___ new day ___ and it don't ___ know white ___ from black, ___

                    Fm   Db   Fm

MOTORMOUTH & ENSEMBLE
___ 'cause the world ___ keeps spin - ning 'round ___ and 'round, and my heart's ___

120

'cause you can't stop the mo-tion of the o-cean or the rain from a-bove. They can try _____ to stop the par-a-dise we're dream-ing of. But you can-not stop the rhy-thm of two hearts in love ___ to stay, _____ **ALL** 'cause you can't stop the beat! _____ Aah, aah, aah.

123

ENJOYED THIS BOOK?

Whether you want to be the next musical *Star of Stage or Screen*, or you just love singing along to your favourite shows... why not check out these fantastic titles...

...available now, these books come complete with PIANO/VOCAL/GUITAR arrangements, FULL LYRICS and superb 'soundalike' BACKING TRACKS on CD!!

A selection of 12 of the most memorable songs from the hit musical **Mamma Mia!** Including...

Dancing Queen
Knowing Me, Knowing You
Mamma Mia
Money, Money, Money
The Name Of The Game
One Of Us
S.O.S.
Super Trouper
Take A Chance On Me
Thank You For The Music
Voulez-Vous
The Winner Takes It All

AM985468

All the songs from Richard O'Brien's monstrous musical Masterpiece
The Rocky Horror Picture Show Including...

Damn It, Janet
Don't Dream It, Be It
Eddie's Teddy
Floor Show
Hot patootie - Bless My Soul
I Can Make You A Man
I'm Going Home
Once In A While
Over At The Frankenstein Place
Planet Schmanet
Rose Tint In My World
Science Fiction - Double Feature
Super Heroes
Sweet Transvestite
The Sword Of Damocles
The Time Warp
Touch-a Touch-a Touch-a Touch Me
Wild And Untamed Thing

AM986766

These titles, plus many more, are available from your local Music Retailer.
In case of difficulty, visit www.musicsales.com or email marketing@musicsales.co.uk

13 songs selected from the hit show **Oliver!** Including...

Food, Glorious Food
Oliver!
Boy For Sale
Where Is Love?
Consider Yourself
Pick-A-Pocket Or Two
It's A Fine Life
I'd Do Anything
Be Back Soon
Oom-Pah-Pah
As Long As He Needs Me
Who Will Buy?
Reviewing The Situation

AM995489

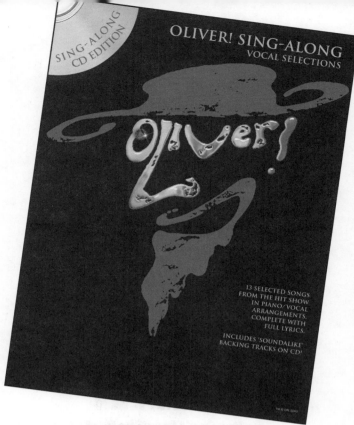

This book is about Freedom, Beauty, Truth, Love and above all else... contains a great selection of FABULOUS songs & medleys from **Moulin Rouge!** Including...

Children Of The Revolution
Come What May
Complainte De La Butte
El Tango De Roxanne
Elephant Love Medley
Lady Marmalade
Nature Boy
One Day I'll Fly Away
Rhythm Of The Night
Sparkling Diamonds
Your Song

AM985457

A selection of the best songs from the hit musical
Les Misérables Including...

A Heart Full Of Love
A Little Fall Of Rain
At The End Of The Day
Bring Him Home
Castle On A Cloud
Do You Hear The People Sing?
Drink With Me
Empty Chairs At Empty Tables
I Dreamed A Dream
In My Life
Master Of The House
On My Own
Stars

MF10138

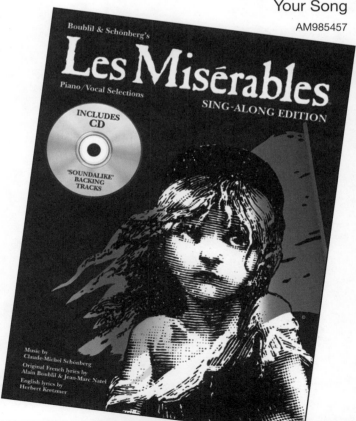

CD Backing Tracks

1. Good Morning Baltimore
2. Nicest Kids In Town
3. Mama I'm A Big Girl Now
4. I Can Hear The Bells
5. It Takes Two
6. Welcome To The 60's
7. Run And Tell That
8. Big Blonde And Beautiful
9. Timeless To Me
10. Without Love
11. I Know Where I've Been
12. You Can't Stop The Beat

All tracks:
(Shaiman/Wittman) Winding Brook Way Music / Walli Woo Entertainment

To remove your CD from the plastic sleeve,
lift the small lip to break the perforations.
Replace the disc after use for convenient storage